RACIAL JUSTICE IN AMERICA
INDIGENOUS PEOPLE

BOARDING SCHOOLS

HEATHER BRUEGL

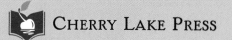

CHERRY LAKE PRESS

Published in the United States of America by Cherry Lake Publishing Group
Ann Arbor, Michigan
www.cherrylakepublishing.com

Reading Adviser: Beth Walker Gambro, MS, Ed., Reading Consultant, Yorkville, IL
Cover Art: Felicia Macheske

Produced by Focus Strategic Communications Inc.

Photo Credits: Library of Congress Prints and Photographs Division, 5, 7, 20, 21, 27; U.S. Bureau of Indian Affairs via Flickr, 9; Minnesota Historical Society, Public domain, via Wikipedia Commons, 11; The Indian Residential School History and Dialogue Centre, 12; *The Minneapolis Journal*, Library of Congress, Chronicling America: Historic American Newspapers, 13; National Archives via Wikimedia Commons, 14, 15; Library of Congress Prints and Photographs Division via Wikimedia Commons, 16; © Darren Thompson, 19; Carlisle Indian School Digital Resource Center, Dickinson College, CC BY-NC-SA 4.0 DEED, 20, 21; Wikimedia Commons, Public domain, 23; Beinecke Rare Book & Manuscript Library, Yale University, Public domain, via Wikimedia Commons, 24, 25; © Hemis/Alamy Stock Photo, 29; © Teko Photography, 31

Cherry Lake Press is an imprint of Cherry Lake Publishing Group.

Library of Congress Cataloging-in-Publication Data

Names: Bruegl, Heather, author.
Title: Boarding schools / by Heather Bruegl, Oneida Nation of Wisconsin/Stockbridge-Munsee.
Description: Ann Arbor, MI : Cherry Lake Publishing, [2024] | Series: Racial justice in America: Indigenous peoples | Includes index. | Audience: Grades 7-9 | Summary: "Learn how education and government policy impacted generations of Indigenous families. Readers will understand the legacy of boarding schools on Indigenous cultures and the resilience of those cultures today. The Racial Justice in America: Indigenous Peoples series explores the issues specific to the Indigenous communities in the United States in a comprehensive, honest, and age-appropriate way. This series was written by Indigenous historian and public scholar Heather Bruegl, a citizen of the Oneida Nation of Wisconsin and a first-line descendant Stockbridge Munsee. The series was developed to reach children of all races and encourage them to approach race, diversity, and inclusion with open eyes and minds"— Provided by publisher.
Identifiers: LCCN 2023043585 | ISBN 9781668937921 (hardcover) | ISBN 9781668938966 (paperback) | ISBN 9781668940303 (ebook) | ISBN 9781668941652 (pdf)
Subjects: LCSH: Off-reservation boarding schools—United States—Juvenile literature. | Indians of North America—Education—Juvenile literature.
Classification: LCC E97 .B74 2024 | DDC 371.829/97—dc23/eng/20231010
LC record available at https://lccn.loc.gov/2023043585

Cherry Lake Publishing would like to acknowledge the work of the Partnership for 21st Century Learning, a Network of Battelle for Kids. Please visit Battelle for Kids online for more information.

Printed in the United States of America

Note from publisher: Websites change regularly, and their future contents are outside of our control. Supervise children when conducting any recommended online searches for extended learning opportunities.

Heather Bruegl, Oneida Nation of Wisconsin/Stockbridge-Munsee is a Madonna University graduate with a Master of Arts in U.S. History. Heather is a public historian and decolonial educator and travels frequently to present on Indigenous American history, including policy and activism. In the Munsee language, Heather's name is Kiishookunkwe, meaning sunflower in full bloom.

CHAPTER 1

What Were Indian Boarding Schools?

Going to school should be a positive experience—learning new concepts and ideas and being with your friends. Those are things that make school fun. However, there were times in history when that was impossible for all students. The era of Indian **boarding schools** is one of these times. The history of Indian boarding schools in the United States is a hard truth. It isn't talked about much. Indigenous peoples are working to change that. It is estimated that 20,000 Indigenous children were in boarding schools by the year 1900. By 1925, that number tripled. Three-hundred sixty seven schools operated in 29 states. We continue to find more information as time goes on.

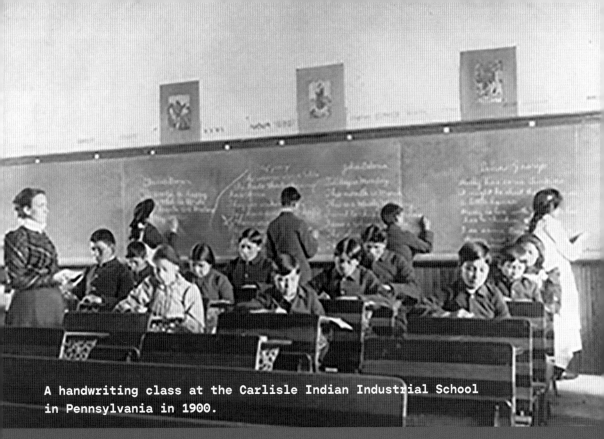

A handwriting class at the Carlisle Indian Industrial School in Pennsylvania in 1900.

Indigenous peoples were the first to live on the land we now call the United States. They lived in tribal nations all over Turtle Island. Turtle Island is an Indigenous name for North America. Indigenous peoples are unique. They have their own culture, traditions, and language. They are part of the land, and the land is part of them. European colonization and the growth of the United States changed things. They separated many Indigenous peoples from their homelands. Over time, the U.S. government forced almost all Indigenous nations onto reservations.

Leaders in the United States saw Indigenous ways of life as a problem. They thought Indigenous people needed to fit in with White society. They passed laws to make this happen. One law broke up tribal land. It restricted how the land could be leased, sold, or inherited. It allowed large pieces of tribal land to be sold to non-native settlers.

The new law gave pieces to individual tribal members. The U.S. leaders wanted individuals to farm small pieces of land themselves. They thought farming would make Indigenous peoples assimilate. To assimilate means to live and behave like another group. In this case, U.S. leaders wanted Indigenous peoples to live like White people.

U.S. leaders thought White, Christian ways of life were better. They wanted to erase Indigenous culture. The federal government funded boarding schools to do this. Indigenous children were sent to boarding schools to force assimilation. Boarding schools were created to eliminate the traditional way of life for Indigenous peoples.

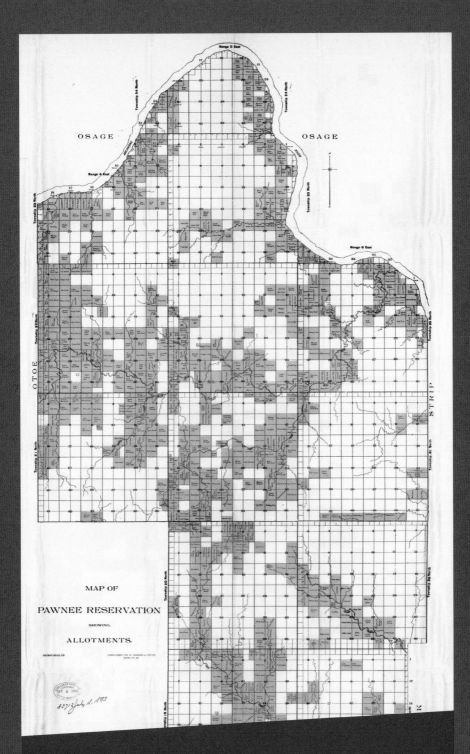

This map shows the allotments of the Pawnee Reservation. The unassigned squares were sold to non-Native settlers.

7

On March 3, 1819, the U.S. Congress passed the Civilization Fund Act. This act gave money to different groups. The groups educated Indigenous children. Some of these groups included Christian missions. The money was meant to support the "civilization process." The federal government considered Indigenous peoples "uncivilized." It did not recognize their human rights or strengths.

In 1824, the Bureau of Indian Affairs (BIA) was created to give money to boarding schools. At the time, the BIA was part of the War Department. Today, the War Department is now known as the Department of Defense. The Bureau of Indian Affairs is now part of the Department of the Interior.

In 1885, Hiram Price, the Commissioner of Indian Affairs, said, "It is cheaper to give them an education than to fight them." The Indian Wars were getting costly. U.S. leaders decided it would cost less to use education to deal with Indigenous peoples. They would use education as a weapon.

Secretary Deb Haaland

The federal government has three branches. The president of the United States is the head of the executive branch. The president runs government departments. The vice president helps. Each department has a secretary that reports to the president. These secretaries are part of the president's cabinet, or advisory council.

Today, there are 15 executive branch departments. Secretary Deb Haaland became Secretary of the Interior on March 16, 2021. She is the first Indigenous cabinet secretary in United States history. She is a member of the Pueblo of Laguna and is a 35th generation New Mexican. For the first time, U.S. federal land and resources are under Indigenous leadership.

CHAPTER 2

What Was Life Like in the Boarding Schools?

People learn their culture as they grow up. They learn from caregivers and elders. The United States government wanted to change what Indigenous children learned. They wanted the children to grow up with no Indigenous culture to pass down to their own children. The boarding school system was going to do just that. It was designed to change an entire people.

While there wasn't a law to send a child to a boarding school, the federal government made it extremely hard not to. The federal government provided food rations to Indigenous families. Often, the land on the reservations could not be farmed and tribal members could not afford farm equipment even if it could be.

A teacher, Mary R. Hyde, with some of her students at Carlisle Indian Training School around 1890.

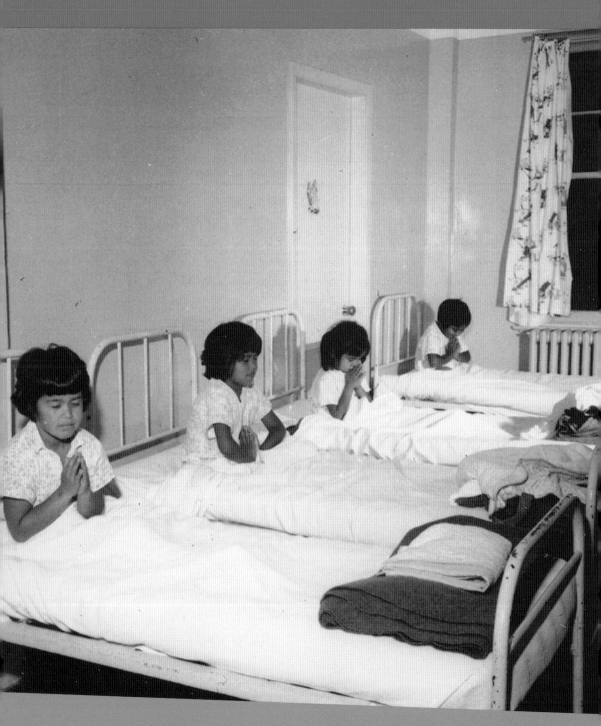

Christianity was central to boarding school life. Indigenous
beliefs and traditions were forbidden.

Indigenous communities were dependent on government food. The government used this food to force families to send children to boarding schools. If families did not, the government withheld food. Without enough food for the younger children still at home, families felt they had no choice but to send their older children to boarding school.

Families that did not send their children were punished in other ways as well. Some families had to pay large fines. Some parents were even arrested if they refused to send their children.

AFTER INDIAN TRUANTS

Superintendent at Oneida Reservation Will Compel School Attendance.

Parents of truant Indians will be arrested under the state statute which provides for compulsory attendance at school.

This *Minneapolis Journal* article from 1906 reported that Indigenous parents would be arrested if children did not attend school.

Once children arrived at a boarding school, life was made even more challenging. Boarding schools for Indigenous children were not gentle places. Children were not there just to learn. Children were there to be changed. The schools themselves were run on child labor. The children always did the farming, cooking, laundry, and repairs for the school under strict supervision. Only part of the day was used to learn to read, write, and do math.

Students farm at Chilocco Indian School in Oklahoma in 1909.

The boarding schools also introduced the European idea of conventional gender roles. This was a foreign concept to Indigenous children. In Indigenous cultures, women were held as equals within the community.

They had political offices and were equal to men— at boarding schools, this way of thinking and behaving was being undone. Boys were taught about farming and construction. Girls were taught how to be ladies and mothers.

Girls' classes included ironing and laundry.

Gender Roles

There are over 500 federally recognized Indigenous tribes in the United States today. Before Europeans arrived, there were many more nations. Some groups of nations shared similar cultures, beliefs, traditions, and languages. But they were all unique.

The roles men and woman had were different in different places. Potawatomi women, for example, were in charge of farming. They planted and tended to crops. They knew about soil, nutrients, and watering needs. Women in Haudenosaunee nations did this as well, as did many others.

Many nations were also **matrilineal**. That meant that land and possessions and even community membership passed down through mothers. In some nations, the women chose the chiefs. It was the chiefs' job to deal with outsiders. Women's roles were very important and their opinions mattered.

CHAPTER 3

How Were Boarding Schools Harmful?

Boarding schools were sites of trauma for many children. Some as young as 4 or 6 were sent. From the moment of their arrival at a boarding school, children were immediately forced to change everything about themselves.

Luther Standing Bear, a notable student at Carlisle, described the arrival at the school: "The civilizing process at Carlisle began with clothes. Whites believed the Indian children could not be civilized while wearing moccasins and blankets. Their hair was cut because, in some mysterious way, long hair stood in the path of our development. They were issued the clothes of white men. High collar stiff-bosomed shirts and suspenders fully three inches in width were uncomfortable. White leather boots caused actual suffering."

Reports and investigations are still being done to learn the full effect boarding schools had on Indigenous children and families.

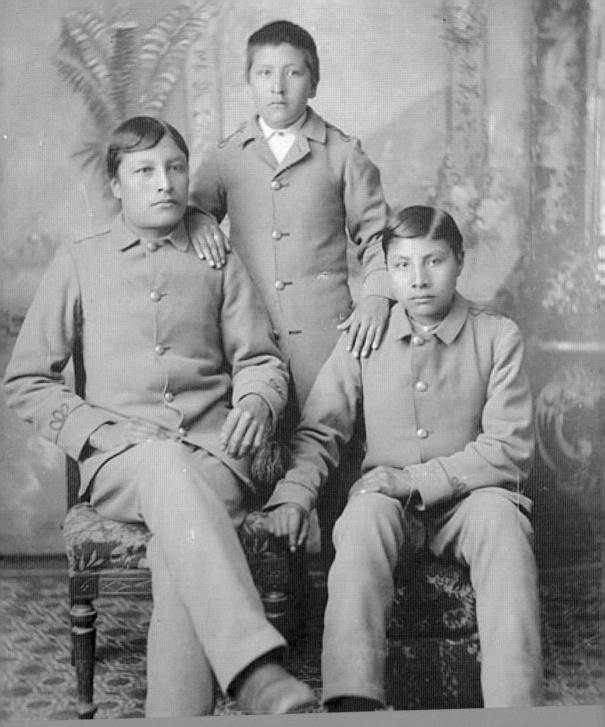

Wounded Yellow Robe (also known as Richard Yellow Robe), Timber Yellow Robe (also known as Chauncey Yellow Robe), and Henry Standing Bear the day after they entered the school on November 15, 1883 (left), and about 6 months later in the spring of 1884 (right).

In many Indigenous traditions, including the Lakota tradition, cutting one's hair symbolized mourning. Wailing and crying lasted well into the first night after children's hair was cut. Children were expected to speak only in English. Indigenous languages were forbidden. Children were given a new English name by choice or assignment. Birth names were no longer used. New names had to come from the Christian Bible. Teachers and staff at the school would also take advantage of Indigenous values. Indigenous children's genuine respect for their elders was used to have them tattle on each other.

Often, the schools were located far away from a child's reservation. For example, Carlisle Indian Industrial School was in Carlisle, Pennsylvania. Many of Carlisle students were Lakota, Cheyenne, and other Plains tribes. This was called distance education. Boarding school and government leaders thought children could only assimilate completely away from their families and culture.

Richard Henry Pratt, the founder of the Carlisle Indian Industrial School, said that the Indian "is born a blank, like all the rest of us . . . Transfer the savage-born infant to the surroundings of a civilization, and he will grow to possess a civilized language and habit."

The Carlisle Indian Industrial School around 1900. Each child was likely far from home.

If you take the child away from everything they know at a young age, you can forever alter that child's world. No matter how far away a school was, children were kept away from their parents. Letters from the parents were taken away, and the schools refused visits by parents.

This photo of Chiricahua Apache children was taken 4 months after they began school in Carlisle.

Student discipline at the boarding schools was harsh. Students who committed severe offenses were court-martialed as if they were in the military. But to be clear, severe offenses could be as minor as speaking in an Indigenous language.

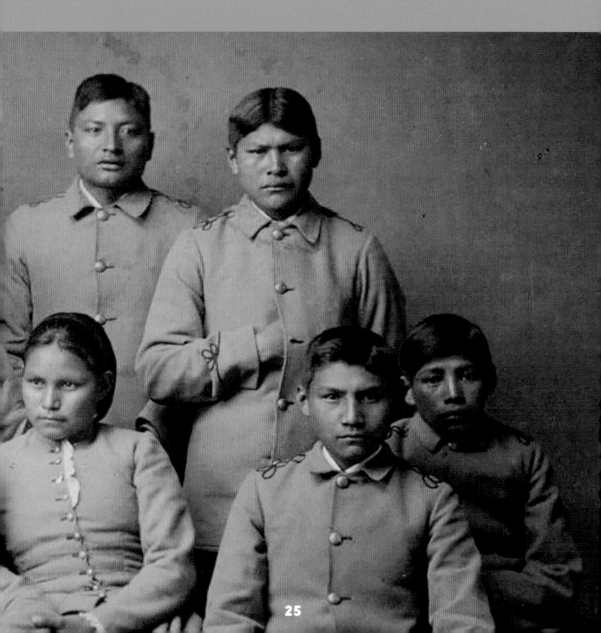

Children would get their mouth washed out with soap if they were caught speaking an Indigenous language. Other times, children were forced into a cold shower and beaten. Solitary confinement, a form of punishment where a person is put all alone in a room, was used to punish children regularly.

Humiliation, physical pain, and invasions of privacy were regular occurrences. In 2022, the U.S. Department of the Interior found that at least 500 Indigenous children had died while attending 19 of the boarding schools funded by the federal government. Some historians estimate as many as 40,000 total children may have died at these schools. These deaths were likely caused by illnesses as well as abuse. Whatever the cause, these children were taken away from their families and never made it back home.

The Carlisle Indian Cemetery includes the graves of children who died at the Carlisle Indian School, far from home and separated from their families.

CHAPTER 4

What Is the Legacy of Indian Boarding Schools?

The trauma students faced at the boarding schools did not end when they left. It did not end when they grew up. It did not end when they got older and became parents. The pain and trauma became **intergenerational** and passed down. The Navajo Code Talkers were heroes credited with helping win World War II. They discussed the effects that boarding schools had on them.

The government that tried to break them of their language later needed that same language to win a war. While in boarding schools, toxic behaviors and traits were learned. The students picked up the use of physical punishment, emotional abuse, and mental abuse. They carried those lessons with them throughout their lives.

Boarding schools also damaged Indigenous family structure. Before colonization, extended family and close family were centers of Indigenous culture. Families lived together. But with boarding, those ties were broken.

The unbreakable code of the Navajo Code Talkers was the key to victory in World War II. The code used the very language boarding schools tried to erase.

Finally, boarding school survivors lost their sense of self and belonging. Where did they belong? Where did they fit in? They were looked at differently by their tribe. They didn't grow up in the community. They were considered outsiders when they returned. But they were still an "Indian" to the rest of society. White society did not accept them, so they didn't fit in there either.

While the boarding school system's trauma continues today, Indigenous people's resilience is stronger than ever. The boarding schools didn't kill everything about Indigenous culture, traditions, and language. Many Indigenous nations and communities have been able to bring back their language, culture, and ceremonies. They have been able to pass them down to a new generation of children. The stories live on. The Ancestors who survived are remembered.

Indigenous children join in powwows across the nation, celebrating their heritage and culture.

EXTEND YOUR LEARNING

BOOKS

Bell, Samantha. *Thanksgiving: The Making of a Myth*. Cherry Lake Publishing, Ann Arbor, MI, 2024.

Dunbar-Ortiz, Roxanne, Jean Mendoza, and Debbie Reese. *An Indigenous Peoples' History of the United States for Young People*. Beacon Press, Boston, 2019.

Loh-Hagan, Virgina. *Stand Up, Speak Out: Indigenous Rights*. 45th Parallel Press, Ann Arbor, MI, 2022.

O'Brien, Cynthia. *Encyclopedia of American Indian History and Culture: Stories, Timelines, Maps and More*. National Geographic Kids, Boone, IA, 2019.

WEBSITES

With an adult, learn more online with these suggested searches.

"National Museum of the American Indian." Smithsonian.

"Native boarding schools." Britannica Kids.

"Taken from Their Families: Native American Boarding Schools." PBS Learning Media.

GLOSSARY

assimilate (uh-SIH-muh-layt) to absorb into another population or group's cultural traditions

boarding schools (BORD-ing SKOOLS) institutions that provide meals and housing for students

colonization (kah-luh-nuh-ZAY-shuhn) the building of settlements on land belonging to others in order to increase a nation's power and/or wealth; often accomplished by armed force

conventional (kuhn-VENCH-nuhl) following agreed upon traditions

food rations (FOOD RA-shuhns) a specific amount of food allowed at regular intervals

generation (jen-uh-RAY-shuhn) a population living during the same time period

Indigenous (in-DI-juh-nuhs) originated from a particular location

intergenerational (in-tuhr-je-nuh-RAY-shuh-nuhl) occurring across generations

matrilineal (ma-truh-LI-nee-uhl) traced through the mother's line

reservations (re-zuhr-VAY-shuhnz) public land set aside for a special group; federally recognized territory under the control of a tribal government

resilience (ri-ZIL-yuhns) overcoming misfortune or change

solitary (SAH-luh-tair-ee) being all alone

traditional (truh-DISH-nuhl) based in customs; ways of doing things passed down from earlier generations

trauma (TRAH-muh) intense mental or emotional harm

INDEX

TITLES IN THIS SERIES

ISBN: 9781499471786
6-pack ISBN: 9781499471793

9 781499 471786